THE

HAND

" I "

WAS

DEALT

BY

PAMELES D. ADAMS

TABLE OF CONTENTS

-Acknowledgements-

This book was a long time in the making, and without the help and encouragement of a host of angels, it would have wandered around forever in "Book Hell", and no one would have ever gotten the chance to witness my transparency, or apply any of my experiences and lessons to their own lives.

First, I want to thank God for letting me make it this far in my life, even though I have had some trials and tribulations, I can still say "I MADE IT!"

This was just a test to see if I would keep going, or if I would break. Again, I say thank you.

I would like to dedicate my book to my three beautiful children: De'Andre, who is the spitting image of me, but in boy form, Donaesh'ah, a pretty and smart young lady. I thank God for her. Last, but not least, there's my baby boy, Donnell Jr (DJ). Whoever came up with the term, momma's boys, must have known that God sent one right to me, and I am forever thankful. They have put up with their crazy mother for years, and I truly want to tell them thank you.

Above all, I offer sincere thanks and love to my parents: Diane Walls, my mother, and Bobby Howze, my father. They raised a phenomenal woman.

I also want to give a special thanks to my stepfather, Robert Walls. He has not only been my stepfather for more than 20 plus years, but he is also my father. He has always been a loving, caring, and understanding caretaker to me and my children over the years, and I am forever grateful to him.

I was raised to believe that I could become anything I wanted to be; all I had to do was set my mind to it, and do it. I love you all, and your support means everything to me.

It is also a pleasure to acknowledge the support, assistance, and guidance of numerous individuals who helped create my story. Thanks to all my friends and family, as well as those who don't know me, but will soon get to know and love me. I am sure there is something you have done for me to help me get to where I am today. Even if it was only a word or two in prayer, I want to say thank you, and I love each and every one of you.

-Author's Note-To The Readers-

This book is intended as a self-help guide for young men and women, especially young ladies around the age of 17. As you read through this book, you will encounter scenarios that may match your life, or someone else's life that you might know. If you haven't encountered any scenarios in this book, just keep living.

Please don't be ashamed, afraid, or embarrassed about anything discussed in this book. Instead, read the stories, the prayers, and the poems carefully, because within them, there could be some insight that will help you, a family member, or a friend, with whatever you are going through. You never know what is going on in someone else's life.

When moving through your life, it's always worthwhile to see things from someone else's point-of-view. Looking at life from just your perspective can make you think some people have it all together, but in reality, you don't know what is going on behind closed doors. The more you understand life, and the good and the bad that comes along with it, the more clearly you can understand other people's perspectives, and show empathy for what they have endured in their lives.

The definition of "**EMPATHY**" is to understand how someone else feels, and to share those feelings.

So as you read the pages that follow, reflect on the information presented to you, because some of my stories may contain nuggets of gold, and information that could prevent you from experiencing heartache and pain.

In the end, my hope is that you can use, or get something from my life experiences, and apply it to your life

today, tomorrow, and for years to come.

-Quote-

"I've come to believe that each of us has a personal calling that is as unique as a fingerprint, and that the best way to succeed is to discover what you love, and then find a way to offer it to others in the form of service, working hard, and also allowing the energy of the universe to lead you."

~ Oprah Winfrey ~

-Thank You God-

I want to thank God for what He has already done for me, and what He is about to do in my life.

I am not going to wait until I see the results, or receive my reward. I am thanking Him now.

I am not going to wait until I feel better, or things look better. I will give Him all the thanks right now.

I am not going to wait until people say they are sorry, or until they stop talking about me, I am thanking Him right now.

I am not going to wait until the pain in my body disappears. I am thanking Him right now.

I am not going to wait until my financial situation improves. I am thanking Him right now. I am not going to wait until the children are asleep, and the house is all quiet. I will thank Him right now.

I am not going to wait until I get that new job I have been waiting for. I am thanking Him right now.

I am not going to wait until I understand every experience in my life that has caused me some type of heartache, pain, or grief. I am thanking Him right now.

I am not going to wait until the journey that I am traveling gets easier, or the challenges are removed. I am thanking Him right now.

I am thanking Him because I am alive today.

I am thanking Him because I have breath in my body.

I am thanking Him because I have made it through the days of difficulties when the devil thought he had won.

I am thanking Him because I have the ability, and the opportunity to do more in my life, and to better myself each and every day.

Each day that I wake up with breath in my body, God is blessing me with another chance at life, and He shows me that He has not given up on me.

I still have to be strong, because at this point in time, I know that the trials I am going through are only a test from God, to see whether I believe in Him or not.

To my readers "I believe in God", and I hope that you do too. I have built up enough faith, strength, hope, and courage to know that I can do all things

through Christ who strengthens me.

Thank You God!

-Introduction-

Everybody has a story. Let me be more specific. Everyone who is divorced has a story. If you ask the husband, he has his version, and if you ask the wife, she has her version...but now, you're going to get my version.

I was going to write openly and honestly about my marriage to a man I loved, and whom I had every intention of staying married to for the rest of our lives. I had the American dream that all girls wish for; the house, the kids, the husband, and the cars, but at that time in my life, at the age of 21, I was missing the most important thing in life...God! It all seemed so right at that age to get married, knowing I didn't know what I was doing. I met a fine young man and fell in love, or what I thought was love. He asked me to marry him, and of course I said yes!

So I started the process as all girls do, because I was excited! So much time and energy had gone into planning my special day. All the waiting ... all the anticipation ... then one day I woke up, and BAM ... my day, October 1, 2001 was finally here!

I was standing at the altar of my little church on the hill, in my pretty little white dress, saying, "I do", in the presence of all my family and friends. This was it! The day both our lives changed forever. The happiest day of my life! We went on from the church to the reception in our limo. It was a full house. Everyone was there to see us! We danced the night away, and had all the food you could eat, all the drinks you can drink, and even had a DJ and photographer there. I had everything a girl could want to make her day special. After the reception, it was time to pack and leave for our honeymoon. Look out Jamaica ... here we come for seven whole days! We had a great time on our honeymoon. On the seventh day, the honeymoon ended and we returned back home to life as Mr. and Mrs. Adams. That's when real life hit me...

I told my husband that I wanted a home before I was 25, and we got it. I was able to experience going to a lot of parcel, seeing nothing there but dirt, and then returning every week and watching the builders build my house. This was the house in which I would raise my children, have family gatherings, cookouts, graduation parties, and so much more. But that was not the way my life turned out. This man gave me all the materialistic things that a woman could want ... big wedding, big ring, the house, the cars, the children, and the money. But there were a lot of things missing, and the most important one was communication. We had little to none, and that drove me crazy!

So now, we had been married for five years, and I still did not know what I was doing. I had questions ... the kind of questions that only my husband could answer. Like ... how do two people commit to each other for a short period of time? At the altar, the preacher said until death do us part. How can we declare til death do us part, but we are apart, and still alive today?

I had no idea how to fix what was going wrong in my marriage, how to make it work, or where to find the glue to put the broken pieces back together again. For someone on the outside looking in, you would have thought that we had the perfect marriage. No honey ... they always told me that you never know what goes on behind closed doors, and that is such a true statement.

Sometimes the strands of the marital relationship just break for reasons known and unknown. We struggled to save our marriage, but after five years, I just gave up without a fight, packed up my things, and walked away from everything, not knowing that in the end, I was hurting myself.

Some of the reasons that lead to my broken marriage were:

- ❖ Lack of common understanding, support and trust
- ❖ Lack of compatibility
- ❖ Lack of mutual cooperation

- ❖ Lack of commitment and sense of responsibility
- ❖ Lack of communication and time
- ❖ Infidelity and breach of trust
- ❖ Inability to effectively cope with the stressors and pressures of marriage
- ❖ Third-person involvement and chaos

Without question, divorce can be one of the most difficult challenges a person faces in their lifetime. Going through my divorce was like riding a roller coaster. One day, I was up so high, and the next day, I would be down so

low. There were even some days when I

was just in the middle.

-Prayer For Marriage-

Lord, I pray that you hold this marriage together when we are facing challenging times.

Lord I pray for peace in my marriage. It feels like everything is coming against us and attacking us.

Lord help me not to give up on my marriage. Help me to stand firm through the challenges.

Lord, I declare and decree what is mine, and I walk in the peace that surpasses all understanding; A peace that you have already promised me.

Lord, take hold of my marriage and don't let go. I know that prayer will make my marriage stronger. I gain clarity when I bring my problems to You.

Humble me in prayer, and strengthen my faith in the journey. Help me to let go and let God.

I speak life into my marriage! The enemy wants to steal, kill, and destroy our marriage. The enemy wants to devour our marriage.

My heart cries out to You Lord. You are the one that I know I can turn to for comfort. I come before you and place our troubled marriage in your hands.

Lord give us a sweetness of speech, eyes only for each other, the discipline to quickly forgive, and to ask for forgiveness.

Give us a desire to work through our struggles and stick it out when we are tempted to flee and turn to someone else.

Give us the willingness to really listen and consider the other person's views. Allow us not to fail to appreciate or to build up one another.

Give us humble hearts.

Deliver us from taking each other for granted. Prevent our eyes from wandering to others.

And please Lord, continue to lead us and guide us in the right direction. Add faith into our union, and shape us into togetherness.

Amen.

-Quote-

"When things break, it's not the actual breaking that prevents them from getting back together again. It's because a little piece gets lost—the two remaining ends couldn't fit together even if they wanted to, the whole shape has changed"

~ David Levithan, Will Grayson ~

-The Beginning-

At first I wondered if I should I write a book; or just leave all this good information that I have in the clouds. I have thought about writing a book about my life since I was 33 years old. Once I turned 34 years old, I started thinking, "So much has happened in my life, that I have to write it down in a book." This book could make me or break me.

Today, I am 39 years young. My name is Pameles (pronounced Pam-me-less). Yes I know it is different and unusual, but that is my real name.

Everybody else is used to Pamela, but not my mother. She wanted something different and I think she got it too. Some people can't even pronounce Pameles, but it's my name – a special name for a special person.

Let me take you back a few years, and walk you through some of the trials and tribulations I have experienced in my life. Where exactly should I begin? The best place to start would be in the beginning, of course.

I am an only child. Being an only child can be good or bad. To me, it was a little bit of both. On one hand, growing up in my house was very hard, but on the other hand, very easy and fun. I have never had to share, never had anyone to fight with, and never had anyone to have those late night talks with. I was, and still am, a very spoiled child. Now people would tell my mother, "I see why she acts the way she acts," and all my mother would say is, "She is my only child."

I grew up in a small town called Great Falls, South Carolina, where there was only one stop light. We had one grocery store, Piggly Wiggly, that everybody called "The Pig". In Great Falls, we had three schools: Great Falls

Elementary, Great Falls Middle, and Great Falls High, also known as "The Devils Den". I attended all three of them, and graduated with my diploma from Great Falls High School.

My elementary and middle school years were great! There were times when I got little bad notes sent home about my behavior, but overall, my formative years were good times. But Lord, when I got to high school...that is when the "Hell" began. I was so ready to get out of high school. I had so many ups and downs until it was not funny. I wish I could go back now and do it over again, or do it the right way. The girls in school always said that I thought I was better than the other girls, or that I thought I was "Miss Goodie Two Shoes". Oh yea, don't let me forget, they said that I thought I was pretty too.

That went on for a couple of years until I got to the eleventh grade. Going into my eleventh-grade year, I started talking to this guy who was about three years older than me. That didn't matter to me though, because I thought I was in love. I would go to school Monday through Friday, and see the "love of my life" on the weekends.

Our puppy love went on for months, until something no mother would wish upon their little girl happened to me. I got pregnant. Yes, you read that right...pregnant.

What a big mistake! You know once us young girls get to high school, as my grandma would say, we'd start "smelling ourselves". I had many different thoughts during this time. I thought about dropping out of school. I even thought about not keeping my baby, but God kept me on the right path.

I remember the day I found out I was pregnant like it was yesterday. It was a Wednesday. I got up, got dressed for school, and my mother reminded me that after school that day, I had an appointment at the Heath Department, I was scheduled to go get birth control, but little did I know, it was too late for that.

The end of the school day came about 3:40 pm. I got on the bus and headed to the Health Department. I arrived at the Health department around 3:55 pm, and signed in. The nurse called my name, and asked me what I was there for. I told her that my mother sent me to get on birth control. That nurse looked at me, and asked me what I thought at that time was the most embarrassing question ever... "Are you sexually active?" I looked her dead in her eyes and said, "Oh no ma'am." She then handed me a cup so that I could give her a urine sample. Once I took that cup into the restroom, my life changed forever.

I placed the urine sample in the window, and came out of the restroom. Once the nurse tested my urine, she looked at me and asked, "Why did you lie to me?"

I looked at her and said, "Lie to you about what?"

She said, "You said that you are not sexually active."

I said, "I'm not."

She looked at me and said, "Well how did you get pregnant?"

I exclaimed, "I don't know, but you better figure it out before my mother gets here!"

Having to pick that phone up and call my mother was like a death of sorts. I dialed her number, and the phone rang twice. When she answered, I exclaimed, "Mom, this nurse said that I'm pregnant!"

She hung the phone up on me. I was sitting in the waiting area and my mind was racing, not knowing how this was going to turn out. Within ten minutes, my mother burst into the door of the Health Department with fire in her eyes. She looked at me. I looked at her. The nurse looked at my mother and said, "Well, what are you going to do?"

My mother said, "She's going to keep it. That's what we're going to do."

I left out of the Health Department that day like a puppy with my tail between my legs. I was so embarrassed. All the way home there was dead silence. I knew my mother was mad at me. However, by 11 pm that night, she wasn't really that mad anymore. She had called all of her friends and told them that she was going to be a grandma. I'm guessing she needed that extra time to get used to the news.

As time went on, I was getting bigger and bigger, but I was still trying to finish high school. I kept going because I didn't want to become a dropout. It was very hard trying to finish school with a newborn, but I knew that I had to do it. Doing homework while a baby is crying is extremely hard.

If I could give anyone a word of advice, it would be to stay safe and protect yourselves. Do not have sex until you are married, and ready to have kids. Most importantly, do not have a child while still in school. Becoming a teenage mother made me quickly realize that I had to grow up and become a woman. I saw that it was time for me to put away childish things. I had to put my education and all my hard work to good use, because now I had a life to take care of other than my own.

Each day, when school was dismissed, I could not ride around town with my friends, go out to eat, or go to the movies. I had to go straight home to do my homework, and to prepare myself, and my baby for the next day. I would have to sleep while the baby was sleeping in order for me to get some rest, so that I could be ready for school the next day.

Despite the odds of being a teenage mother, I made it! Yes I finished high school with my diploma and my baby in tow!

-Prayer-

-For teenage mothers and fathers-

Just a little note to let all of you teenage mothers and fathers know that I am praying for you.

I was a teen mother myself, I was sixteen when my boyfriend and I got pregnant, and seventeen when I had my first son.

Just remember God never puts more on us than we can bear. If you ever need someone to talk to, God is a "Great Listener".

Father God, I come to you today to intercede on behalf of all teenage mothers and fathers.

Thank you for watching over them. God, sometimes they get so preoccupied with life, that they forget to take the time to tell you how much they appreciate all that You do for them.

Thank you God for guiding them in the right direction, for helping them to make successful decisions, and for seeing them through all their hard times. God help them to understand that with You all things are possible if they just believe.

Please continue to prove it to them, and to let them know that their help truly cometh from only You.

I beseech you for strength and for wisdom that they will be able to endure all situations, and be able to handle it in a way that would bring glory to Your name.

God help them to always call upon You and only You. In the name of Jesus. Amen!

-Jesus Came to Set Them Free-

There are so many people that come in and out of your life daily, and then there are the people who you are born unto. The Lord blessed me with a loving, caring, giving, and understanding grandmother.

Now let me tell you about my grandmother. Mary Perry. She was known to all as Bad Mamma Jamma, and she was the best grandmother that a grandchild could ever ask for. She would give you her last dime, unless she was going to play Bingo. According to her,

Bingo was her boyfriend! My grandmother loved to go play Bingo, and she would play Thursday through Sunday if she had the money.

When I was a little girl, I would sit with my grandmother as she got dressed, and I would ask her, "Grandma, where you are going all dressed up?" She would reply, "I'm going to see my boyfriend."

My grandmother also loved to go to the Goodwill on Tuesdays. Tuesday was Senior Citizens Day, and she could get an extra ten percent off. She would come back with all kinds of stuff! Unfortunately, she didn't pass along that trait to me, because if I were to go to the Goodwill, I wouldn't be able to find a thing. I guess it's an old lady thing.

Bad Mamma Jamma loved all of her grandchildren very much. Sometimes I think she loved us more than she loved her own children. She would always give us our way no matter what.

My grandmother worked hard all her life, and I'm glad to say that trait did rub off on me. One of the reasons why I work so hard, is because I want to be just like her. She started working in New York City as a nurse, then she moved to South Carolina with her children, and

South Carolina is where she stayed until God called her home in March of 2009. Mary Perry lived to be an old lady in her late eighties, and she always had more money than me, and I'm a young lady with a full- time job.

My grandmother and I were very close. I would always tell people that she was my mother, and that my mother was my sister. When I would stay with my grandmother for the weekends, we would go to Bingo together, and that is where we would spend our Friday and Saturday nights. I would ride the bus from school to her house on Friday, and go home on Sunday if I wanted to. If I didn't want to go home, on Mondays, I would catch the bus from her house to school.

My grandmother was the best. We did everything together. Now that she's gone, I really miss her. I thank God that she was able to see me bring three beautiful children into this world. She was right there with me for all three of my births. She would take me back and forth to my doctor appointments and my checkups, and she was front and center when I delivered my children. Bad Mamma Jamma would treat my kids the same way she treated me when I was a little girl. She would give them money, and she would keep them for me, because she did not believe in letting someone else keep my kids. Even though she said that they were busybodies, she would never call them bad, and at her age she could handle them all, except my baby boy.

I recall coming home from work one day, and my grandmother had tied my baby to a chair. When he saw me pull into the driveway, he picked up the whole chair up and jumped to the door! He had ran around her house all day, breaking stuff and tearing things down until she couldn't take it anymore. He even went into the refrigerator, grabbed the milk and poured it all over the floor! I know she wanted to hang him. Those were the days with her.

My grandmother stayed on the go. She always thought she was a young chick. Bad Mamma Jamma always told people she was eighteen years old. Her age never changed, even though she was born in 1926.

My grandmother would get her check on the third of each month. She would go out early in the morning, around 8 am, and head to the bank to cash her check, because she wasn't one of those ladies that believed in direct deposit. Then she would start making her rounds to pay all her bills. While in the process of paying all her bills, she would always buy me something, whether it was food, an outfit from her favorite place, the Goodwill, school supplies, or just things she knew I needed or wanted. She did not like to see me cry for anything. I was able to share twenty-eight wonderful years with my grandmother before God called her home. I truly miss her presence and her spirit, but I know that God needed her more.

It hurt me so bad when my grandmother passed, and it felt like God took everything from me. She was my everything! I would go to my grandma for everything, including advice. I even went to her for advice about my marriage. You see, my grandmother came from the old days and she would always say, "If he is not hitting you, you better stay there." She would also say, "As long as those bills getting paid, and he is taking care of those babies, everything else will be ok."

I would respond by telling her, "Grandma, marriage is not as easy as it was back when you were married."

Now that she is gone, I have no one to go to for that good old school advice. My grandmother made me into such a strong woman. She was such a precious gift to me.

Rest in Peace Mary Perry.

My life since my grandmother has been gone has truly been a struggle, but I fight each and every day to make it. There's no wisdom from her to live by, and no comforting words to help me get through the day. What is a grandchild to do? So now, I make it a point to live each day to make her proud of me.

Another person that I loved and lost was my aunt Willie Mae. She was the best aunt that a girl could ask for. Aunt Willie Mae always gave me money, she taught me how to cook, and would protect me from getting spankings if I did something bad. Aunt Willie Mae also babysat my children for me, and she was the one that told me that my babies weren't going to be babies long. Aunt Willie Mae was everything to me.

The night I got that phone call from Uncle Fred was the night my life

changed forever. He called and said that
we needed to come to his house as soon
as possible, because there was something
wrong with Willie Mae. By the time I got
there, I saw the ambulance, and lots of
people just standing around and looking.
I really didn't know what to expect, but
once I got out of the car, I ran into the
house and froze.

My aunt was lying on the floor
and the paramedics were working on her
and trying to resuscitate her. It was
heartbreaking to me to realize that night
was going to be the last time I got to call
her on the phone. I knew at that point

that my aunt had passed on to heaven to be with her mother, but they still took her to the hospital, and they continued to work on her the whole way there. The paramedics gave their all trying to save her. I really do thank them for their hard work, and their faith to not give up. They didn't know that she was leaving behind a niece that needed her.

All of the family was gathered at the hospital when the head doctor called us into the family room to tell us that Willie Mae had passed. That finalized everything for me. I could remember all the times we shared, and there were so many years to remember.

Aunt Willie Mae loved me, but most of all she loved herself some Fred. They had been together for more than 20 years. I know Uncle Fred misses her, and so do I. I sit to myself sometimes and I wonder what she is doing up there in heaven. Is she enjoying herself with her mother, her brother, and her nephew? Is she playing those lottery tickets, drinking her Pepsi, and smoking those Newport cigarettes? One thing I do know is that Willie Mae has no more worries.

I truly think my loved ones that passed on before me are all up in heaven watching over me, to make sure that I am still doing what is right, and taking care of my family. Rest in Peace Aunt Willie Mae.

-Photos-

My Grandmother
Mary Perry AKA
"Bad Mamma Jamma"

My Aunt
Willie Mae Perry

-Prayer-

-For Strength When Grieving-

Father, despite my heart being so heavy and my spirit being in mourning, please help me to process my loss.

Help me to move forward in my life.

Help me to welcome joy and laughter in place of this pain and sadness.

I know that I am going to miss my loved one, who had been my strength and my joy for so long,

Lord I thank You for the precious times we had together.

God, please give me the courage and strength to face all the days ahead, and to help me get through this thing called "life".

Please broaden my mind so that I can accept all things as they come. I know that when I can't pray, You are still listening to my heart.

Continue to bless me so that I may be a blessing to others.

Keep me strong so that I may help the weak.

Keep me uplifted so that I may

have words of encouragement for others.

I pray for those who will read this

prayer, that they may let You know that

they need You today, tomorrow, and

forever more.

Amen!

-Single with THREE-

After getting divorced, some days are more emotionally trying than others. I may be single right now, but like the old gospel song says, "As long as I've got King Jesus, I don't need nobody else." Some of you may recognize that old gospel song. With Jesus in my life, I have no worries, but sometimes, I think having a man in my life is trouble within itself.

Some men will have most women out here worrying about what time he is coming home, what he is really out there doing in those streets, or who he is doing it with. However, to me, being a single woman is a perk, because I don't have to worry about things like that.

I'm not going to lie though... sometimes what hurts the most is being single and raising three children on your own. I have three beautiful children: two boys and one girl. I thank God for them every day. It is a blessing to get up in the morning, see my children look at me, and know that I am doing all that I can to make sure that they are safe and at peace. That really helps me make it through my day, because I know they need me more than anything else in this world. I have to stay strong so that I am able to give them everything they need in life. I don't want them to fall short due to the downfalls I've had in my life.

I get up every morning at 5:30 am, get myself dressed, make breakfast, wake my children up by 6:00 am, make sure that they get dressed for school, and then I am off to work from 8:00 am to 5:00 pm, to make money and provide for them.

I want to give my children a good education, and the things that I didn't have in my childhood. Even though it gets hard, I just ask God for a little bit more energy to make it, and to keep going.

When my boys want to play basketball, or football, or run track, or when my little girl wants to cheer, I just have to look up and see where my help comes from. I really have a hard time with that type of stuff, because boys really need a male figure in their lives. When it comes to sports, and other manly things, I just do the best that I can as a woman.

Right now, I have a home for my children that is safe, we have a car to get around in, we have food to eat, and most importantly, we have Jesus. And Jesus will see to it that we are continually blessed.

Some days though, being a single mother hurts. Some days, I cry until I fall asleep. I look in the mirror and ask God, "Why Lord? Why me?"

I never thought something like this could happen to me. Once upon a time, when I was married, I had the American dream: the house, the kids, the husband, and the cars.

Just to give you a better understanding about my life as a single mother each day...I am a Teacher, Counselor, Taxi, Doctor, Best Friend, Cook, Nurse, Supporter, and the list goes on and on. But I wouldn't trade it for anything in the world. I love being a mother! My children are a blessing, and a gift. My relationship with them is one that will never end, and my love for them will never die.

Raising my kids is easier now than when I first became single, because I had a praying grandmother who taught me the true meaning of living life. She also warned me in advance that every day was not going to be like Sunday. I treasure the lessons that she taught me, and all

the advice that she gave me, because it

helped me to be the best mother that I

can be, and made being single with three

a little less overwhelming.

-A Prayer for Parents-

Dear Lord,

Raising children is an amazing process, and I thank You for trusting in me to do this job.

I thank you for their life, health and strength. I know they are a gift from You and they are a blessing to me. I thank You for trusting me with Your precious gifts.

I need Your strength and wisdom to train them up in the way that they should go. Give me patience and a joyful heart. Let me be an example of Your love and forgiveness.

God I thank you for increasing my finances so I can afford to provide my children with food, clothing, and shelter.

Lord, I thank You for keeping me safe from all the hurt, harm, and danger that was around me.

Lord I thank You for showing me the truth about certain people, and removing the ones that were not supposed to be in my life.

Bless me to continue to be a good role model for my children.

Thank you Father for the honor of being a parent.

Amen!

-The Love I have for my Mother-

Let me tell you about my mother. My mother's name is Diane, and she is one of the most important people in my life. My mother is the baby of six children, unlike myself as an only child. My mother was originally born in Brooklyn, New York, where she lived until she was about twelve years old, and then moved to South Carolina with my grandmother.

The love that I have for my mother is second after the love I have for God. Without my mother, I would not have made it this far in life. My mother and I have been through so many experiences together, good and bad, that have tested our relationship. I was an only child, and I was also wild in school. My mother would have to come to my school so much to see about me until they offered her a job there! There were many days that I thought I was grown, and did not want to listen to what she had to say. And of course, the ultimate test to our relationship was when I got pregnant while still in high school.

Despite our issues, we have always managed to come out on top from the devil's mess. That is what the power of prayer can do. I love my mother. She has instilled many values in my life.

My mother, who was also a single mother, raised me as her only child, and shaped me into the godly woman that I am today. My upbringing also set the foundation for how I raise my own children.

My mother would go hard each and every day to show me that she was determined to provide me with the very best. She also made sure that I had the same opportunities as all of the other kids.

My mother never held me back from doing anything I wanted to do. She let me experience life, but was right there by my side no matter what, right or wrong. My mother and I have always had a very open and trusting mother-daughter relationship. When I first told my mother that I was pregnant, I really thought I was going to die at an early age. I thought my mother was going to kill me, but after a few hours went by, and she was able to clear her head, I think she finally forgave me, and we have been fine ever since.

These days, my mother is dealing with a lot in her life. She lost her mother and her sister, two very important people in her life. She has shared with me that when you lose your mother, it feels like your whole life is over. Losing her mother took everything out of her. I treasure and honor my mother to the fullest, because I don't want to know what life would be like without her. So for those of you that still have your mother in your lives, please honor and treasure her while she is still living.

I Love you Mommy!

-A Prayer of Covering-

Lord, thank you for all the
blessings You have bestowed upon me.
Most of all, thank You for these
wonderful children that You have blessed
me with.

Having children makes a mother
feel so vulnerable. Of course, I love my
children, and while I cannot control
everything they do, I can surely pray over
everything concerning them.

There are other times when I
struggle to give them the freedom to live,
to grow, and to learn, because all I can

remember was that it was just yesterday when I was putting bandaids on their scrapes, and a hug and kiss was enough to make the nightmares go away.

Lord, there are so many ways of the world that terrify me. I ask that you guide their footsteps as they walk in this world on their own.

Help me offer the right advice and set the right rules for my children to help them be the people of God You desire them to be.

In your Holy name, Amen!

-Inspiration-

This is for all the single ladies in the world, and single men, especially the ones that have children. I know you may feel like the world and the people of the world are against you. Maybe everything that you are doing, or are trying to do, is just not turning in your favor. At these times, you have to **P.U.S.H.**

P-ray

U-ntil

S-omething

H-appens

Some of the problems that you are dealing with in life may have you all over the place, making you feel like you can't function in your own body. I am here to let you know that God is still in control.

Sometimes God gives the biggest battles to the weak, just to see how you will deal with it. Will you give up and throw in the towel, or continue to trust in Him? He is watching to see if you know how to walk by faith and not by sight.

In the beginning, I too walked by sight and not by faith. There were times in my life, when I would even say that

God had left me all alone knowing that I couldn't do this by myself.

A great scripture that I used to help me through the times I struggled with my faith is Galatians 2:20 New International Version (NIV). It reads, "I have been crucified with Christ and I no longer live, but Christ lives in me. The life I now live in the body, I live by faith in the Son of God, who loved me and gave himself for me."

I pray that these words will inspire you to face your battles, and I hope that you continue to pray to the Lord for the understanding you need to face any

challenges that life may bring your way.

-Connection with God-

Do you have a personal

relationship with God? Having that

connection has the potential to help you

grow in ways that you never thought you

could. The time you spend researching,

crying, and figuring out why your life is not the same as someone else's life, you can use that time to connect with God and discover His plan for your life.

How can you connect with God? Fall on your knees and ask God to help you. Once you ask God for help, make Him your top priority. Put Him before everything and everyone else.

Make changes in your life to allow yourself to spend time with God so that you can hear from Him. It will be hard to hear from Him in the beginning, and sometimes, you will feel that He is not listening to you, but don't give up.

Simplify your life as much as possible, so you are not too exhausted to invest private time and energy into your prayers.

Whenever you encounter challenges, view them as opportunities. Ask God to give you more faith to keep you strong through the challenges. Clearly identify what you're seeking when you pray. Don't be vague. Tell God exactly what you hope to receive.

Open your bible and find verses that fit your situation, problems, or whatever is going on in your life. Write those verses on post-its, and put them up all around you, so that it can be a daily reminder of what God will do in your life. This is what He promises to us in His Word.

Instead of relying on anyone else to tell you what God wants for your life, start a direct conversation with Him. Have a relationship with Him. Tell Him what is on your mind. Tell Him your concerns. Ask for what you need, and for what you want. Pray for the needs of others.

Finally, believe that what you ask for will be answered. You don't have to be shy about your relationship with the

Father. You can be confident of God's love for you, and His desire to bless you.

This is something I found on Facebook and it has really helped me along the way, I pray that it will do the same for you.

LOST	FRIENDSHIP
Isaiah 4:10	1 Corinthians 15:33
Psalm 91:11	Proverbs 13:20
2 Timothy 4:17	Proverbs 17:17
Jeremiah 1:5	Proverbs 18:24

CONFUSED	PURPOSE
Matthew 7:7	Jeremiah 29:11
2 Timothy 2:7	Proverbs 16:9
1 Corinthians 14:33	John 15:16
Isaiah 40:31	Romans 8:28

BROKEN - HEART	WAITING ON GOD
Psalm 34:17-18	Isaiah 30:18
Psalm 147:3	Psalm 27:14
Psalm 73:26	Psalm 37:4

PATIENCE	LOVE
John 13:7	Colossians 3:14
Ecclesiastes 7:8	1 Peter 4:8
Psalm 37:7	1 Corinthians 13:13
Isaiah 40:31	1 Corinthians 13:7

NEEDING DIRECTION	STRENGTH
Psalm 73:21-26	Psalms 16:8
Proverbs 3:6	1 Corinthians 16:13
Proverbs 20:24	Joshua 1:9

-CONGRATULATIONS-

You have made it to the last chapter! You have read about some of the trials and tribulations, good times and bad times I've experienced in my life. If none of these situations have happened to you yet, just keep on living, and some of these situations will come your way.

Now comes the hard part— applying what you have learned in these chapters to the realities of your everyday life. You see, it's easy to see another person's life, and think you know their story, but it's different when the story is yours.

Starting today, do whatever it takes to pray more, work to achieve the goals you want, and stay strong. Don't worry about the mistakes you made yesterday, or the day before, and don't fret about the uncertainties of tomorrow. Just focus on living your life to the fullest, or as the kids say today, living your best life!

Most importantly, stop following the crowd and be yourself. Stand out, and in some cases, don't be afraid to stand alone.

So make today your new beginning. Focus on the values you hold, and speak encouraging words and life unto yourself. Read your bible for understanding, and remember that you are great, just the way you are. Thank you for reading my story.

-ABOUT THE AUTHOR-

Pameles D. Adams, is the only

child of Diane Walls & Bobby Howze Jr.

In addition to being a writer,

Pameles is very passionate about her

work. She enjoys her job, looks forward

to going to work each day, and takes

pride in everything she sets her mind to.

She cannot believe that she gets paid to

do something that she really likes to

do...talking!

Pameles holds an Associate's

Degree in Paralegal Studies. She loves

traveling, shopping, and attending her home church—Pine Grove Baptist Church. Most of all, she enjoys family time with her children, De'Andre, Donaesh'ah, Donnell Jr., and her grandson Justin.

Pameles covers topics, such as single motherhood, education, break-ups, death, etc., with the hopes that her life experiences will allow others to relate to the most relevant issues of today.

Made in the USA
Columbia, SC
02 February 2021